Move Maker's Handbook

"Lessons Learned from an Entrepreneur and Dreamer"

RYAN "JENKS" JENKINS

© 2014 By Ryan Jenkins

Norfolk, VA

MOVE MAKER'S HANDBOOK INTRO

If you are interested in being an entrepreneur and are reading this intro, that means your dreams are TOO BIG to fit into 8hr work days and 40hr work weeks. It's time to stop thinking you can do what people who work 40 hour work weeks do. THAT'S NOT YOU ANYMORE!! Now you have to think like someone who is a DREAM CHASER. Because the reality check is, YOU ARE!! You have to think like someone who doesn't have time in his schedule, BUT MAKES time in his schedule. God gives every man 24 hours in a day, YOU HAVE TO MAKE YOURS COUNT. You can't waste time, you have things to do and dreams to accomplish. The people that sit around and gossip don't have businesses. They aren't chasing their dreams, BUT YOU ARE.

Your time is more valuable to you!! You have more to accomplish in 24 hours so that it may reap great benefits in another 24 hours. You can't ask, "Why I can't do this", "Why I can't do that" or "Why I can't go there?" YOU DON'T HAVE TIME!! If you want to do all that, don't chase dreams and then you will have the time. If you don't want to work during the day, work at lunch, work when you get off work, work while you're driving home, work when you get home, work late at night and just WORK HARD trying to make things work, well STOP TRYING TO ACHIEVE YOUR DREAMS NOW!! It's not going to be easy. This will be your NORM!!

You can make time for family, faith and YOU, but you will have to prioritize. Prioritizing your life in pursuit of your dreams will require work too! Going after a dream can be demanding and it will require great SACRIFICE. It may require working long days, long nights, and most weekends. This is what it is!! Anything WORTH going after will come with sacrifice. The question is, HOW MUCH are you willing to sacrifice? So if you want to do what other people are doing, stop going after your dream and do what they are doing. However, understand those people aren't going very far. If you have read this intro and are still willing to PUSH FORWARD, READ ON, GET ON YOUR GRIND and let's figure out how you can make today's 24 hours more productive than yesterday. NOW it's time to CATCH YOUR DREAM!!

"THE SUCCESS SECRET"

PASSION SALES PRODUCTS

Who wants to buy a product they don't believe in? You have to believe in what you are selling. The first sale you have to make is YOU. Yes, you are your first buyer. If you can't create a pitch that sales the product to you, why would anyone else buy it? You have to have a great argument. Behavioral Psychologist, *John B. Watson* believed that fear, rage and love was the key to good advertising. (Watson, 1999) You have to use this theory to make your customer feel like they need this product. You have to tell how this product will make life easier. Think about it, you have to convince the customer to be willing to come off their hard earned money for your product.

Writer Geoffrey James, from the website INC., stated that one mistake business's make is not keeping the ball in their court. (James, 2012) Some businesses let the customer take the next action. For example, some companies ask the potential customer to call the company when they are ready buy. If you say, "I will call you next week to set up a meeting", this keeps you in control of the sale. Geoffrey James also stated the importance of following up. (James, 2012) You have to do what you say you are going to do to gain the customer's trust and to keep your sale. Trust is the key to any good relationship and sales relationships too.

When I am selling a book, I make you feel like I enjoyed writing the book, because I did!! I believe in the product I produce. I know the lessons I have learned in my life can help others. And I make the person buying the book feel like that person is them. When asked about motivational speaking, I am excited to talk about the various subjects I can cover. This is because I enjoy what I do. You have to have the same passion about your product.

I have an exercise for you. Go to the mirror with your product in hand (i.e. a picture of product, flyer, etc) and try to explain the product to yourself. Tell yourself how wonderful the product is and how it can help you. If you say this is too hard, how can you look others in their faces and tell them about your product, when you can't tell yourself? Ok, let's make it a little easier. Go to an empty room in your home and act like you have an audience. Now tell your audience about your product. Also, act like they are asking you questions. I call this "shadow boxing". When a boxer shadow boxes, he throws punches and also acts like punches are being thrown back at him. You have to do the same!! This exercise will prepare you for selling your product and answering questions about your product. Even if you have been selling your product for a while, this is still a good technique. It will help you sharpen your skills. You can get reinvigorated about your product!!

DON'T DO WHAT'S POPULAR, DO WHAT'S PRODUCTIVE

Many entrepreneurs try to do what other entrepreneurs are doing. However, that model doesn't work for everyone. One person may be gifted to do business a certain way while another may not. Some people are great at social media and that's the key to their sales. Nevertheless, you don't have to get a Twitter account, Facebook account or ABCDEF account. This may cause more confusion than help. It is amazing how many people are doing VERY well in business without all the social media. Some companies don't even have websites, but are raking in the doe!! Yes, without social media, your buyers are limited in what they can learn about your product, but it can be done.

I am a strong believer that you have to do what works best for you. Some people use all their time on social media while some people are out there meeting people. If meeting people has been working for your business, then keep doing it!! You should always play on your strengths. Some people using social media are not good communicators when meeting people face-to-face. However, I believe every entrepreneur can work to benefit his business and his customers. If you are not good with social media, link up with someone who is. They may show you some shortcuts or you can make an arrangement for them to do the social media part of your business. If you are not the best communicator face-to-face, link up with someone who is a good communicator. They may share some good advice or you may be able to arrange for them to become your face-to-face salesperson.

We have to do what works for us. I am a good communicator face-to-face. I enjoy talking with people and discovering their needs. That is my strength!! I sell plenty of books face-to-face versus on-line. However, I know other authors that aren't good speaking face-to-face but they make plenty of sales online. That doesn't mean I am going to change my plan and increase my on-line time.

That does not excite me. But speaking face-to-face does!! Since face-to-face sales work for me, that is what I will do. In addition, I will perfect how to increase my face-to-face sales. It is productive for me even though it may not be the most popular.

"Your past tragedies can provoke your future triumph."

THE SHINY DIME

One important subject to talk about in starting a business is overhead. Overhead is defined as business expenses that are not chargeable to the work or product of the business. Examples are rent and insurance. Overhead are the expenses you have to pay before you get to your profit. If you have too much overhead, you will end up in the negative or some people say the "red". I think overhead is overlooked a lot of the time. For a new entrepreneur, you are just thinking about how much you can make by selling your product. But that is only half the battle. It cost you something to create the product or house the product. This is the overhead. If you deduct what it cost you to create the product and package the product from how much you made, that is the true profit. Your small business could have made $2 million dollars last year, but your expenses were $3 million. This leaves you $1 million in the whole. The point is, just because you are making money does not mean you are being profitable. A lot of profitable businesses went out of business this year. I had profitable businesses that went out of business. The overhead was too high!!

In one business I had, I spent a lot of my budget trying to make the business look nice. I paid for nice furniture, pictures and other items. Unfortunately, that didn't make much difference in the business. I called that having a "Shiny Dime", but it was still only worth 10 cents. These expenses did not bring more people to my business. I should have spent the money in what could have potentially brought more clients to the business. Instead, I was concerned about what the business would look like when customers came in. Appearance is important, but it's not everything. Yes, I put the cart before the horse. I had to get the people there first.

In Jean Chatzky's book *Money Rules*, she says, "The Jones are in debt."(Chatzky, 2012) I was trying to make my business look like the Jones' business but I was not properly managing the debt I was occurring. I should have invested more time in advertising and more energy in marketing my products and services. Now, I am not telling you to spend your last penny on advertising!! I believe advertising works differently for different businesses and industries. You have to try various avenues and see what works for you. Look around and study the advertising strategies of other companies. Next, ask them if it is working. Of course, the best advertising is word-of-mouth but sometimes you have to go a little further.

BUSINESS PARTNERS: INTENT AND REASON

I have learned that going into a business for the right reason is important. I have tried to start a business just to make money, but that plan didn't work. I was so focused on making money that I didn't have the passion to endure the rough times. Every business will have challenges. It may be in the beginning or maybe in the middle that leads to an end. Just like life, challenges do happen but how you deal with the challenges determines how your future plays out.

In my new wisdom, I found 2 partners named "Intent and Reason". They became my counselors!! The question they asked me was "Why do you want to start this business?" If the answer was for money, they were "OUT" like blown light bulbs. They would not partner with me unless there was something meaningful behind my business. Like stated in Forbes, "vision mismatch is a partnership killer" and Intent and Reason already knew that. (Lindner, 2008) The other question was "If the business wasn't going so well, would I keep going?" If you have the right motives in your business, you will keep going. However, I am not saying go bankrupt three times with the same business and same business strategy. Something would definitely have to change!!

Here's my point, you need to have a purpose behind starting a business. You have to have a personal interest in the creation of your business. Maybe it fills a need that is close to your heart. Maybe the business is that thing you love doing and you would do for free if you didn't have bills to pay. Intent and Reason show up when the business is more than something to do. So if you are thinking about starting a business or already have, I would suggest you have a consultation with Intent and Reason before you go any further. The consultation will be free, but it will cost you a lot of truth and honesty.

INTENT   REASON

"Don't believe who people say you are. Live and own who YOU say you are."

CHANGING CIRCLES

I have learned that when you pursue an entrepreneurial endeavor, your circle of friends will change intentionally or unintentionally. First, I would tell anyone who is going to start a business to find someone who is already in that form of business. Set up a meeting with them and ask them questions. Ask them questions like: How did you start your business? What are some of the challenges in the business? How did you overcome the challenges? What challenges do you still face? These are just a few questions that will help you get started.

Now there is a rumor that most business owners won't talk to you because they will see you as competition. But that's not all true!! Most entrepreneurs like to talk about themselves and their business (I'm guilty). Also, they may not see you as competition because you can't do what they do like they do it!! Oh, did I mention it takes confidence to be an entrepreneur.

Building relationships is very important in any business. The people you meet could be your next customers or they may help you find new customers. I am definitely a person that believes in building relationships. I am not saying we have to talk every day, but we should be able to call each other to share information when needed. A hello every now and then doesn't hurt either. Build a phonebook of people you have met and what they do. Their services could become more meaningful to you in the future. Or you may know someone that needs their services and you will be able to refer them.

Here are 3 outcomes to good relationship building. First, the person that needed the service reaches their goal. Second, the person with the business just gained a new client. Third, you become a reliable resource to both parties. What a marriage in business!! Now don't go and start a consulting company based solely on this information!! Sometimes you have to act as a consultant to build good relationships. If consulting is your business, then you need to use your resources to help others and figure out how you can get paid for it. But like I said before, you have to have passion for consulting. Not just trying to make a quick buck.

I read a book entitled "Networking with the Affluent" that discussed how helping others could help you. It gave examples of how helping other businesses or groups reach their goals, may create opportunities for you indirectly. (Stanley, 1997) By sharing your knowledge to help other causes, some people start to wonder, "Who is this guy who is willing to help us for free and what type of business does he have?" People like to work with people with a good heart. A good heart is like a magnet, it pulls people in. As you help other people reach their goals, you meet new people in various industries. This is a great opportunity to add to your business phonebook. I will give you an example. Suppose you have a Life Coaching business and you want to write a book one day. At the same time, you decide to help a non-profit business for people with cancer. You conduct a workshop on creating a better life for cancer survivors as part of their fundraiser. This may be something they never thought of doing.

While in the meetings, you meet people from all walks of life because cancer affects everyone. By doing this service to help, you happen to meet a publisher that supports the cause too. He or she may be intrigued by the workshop you gave, and as a result wants to publish the book that is in your heart. All of this happened because you decided to help someone else reach their goal. Now if you take this idea, I will be looking for my royalty check in the mail for my consulting services!! Just kidding, but it is a good idea. Think about other ways you can help and build better relationships. As you grow in relationships, watch your circle begin to change.

PUT IT IN MOTION

I had an idea but that wasn't good enough,
I had to put it on paper to make sure it wasn't a bluff.
I wrote and wrote until it was all out,
Now I had to put it in motion like I was an Eagle Scout.

Next I had to come up with a plan,
No idea breathes life if it's not worked out in your mind and with your hands.
Then I was worried about not having the finances to do the business,
But I knew I had resources, so all I needed to do was handle my business.

I made some phone calls and my dream became clearer,
One resource lead to another resource like UPS packages
and God was the deliverer.
I knew then my vision was closer in reach,
It's amazing an idea can become a reality you can see.

A few weeks later it was all done,
But I knew I was going to achieve my goal before the first phone had rung.
You have to believe in yourself and the Giver of promotion,
With faith and some hard work, you too can put it in motion.

"As you climb your challenges like mountains, you will begin to see from a viewpoint you have never seen before."

LOOK LIKE A FOOL

To have a successful business, you must be willing to look like a FOOL. FOOL meaning "Following Only One Lead." And that one lead is YOU. You have to be willing to follow what is in your heart and not the hearts of those who are too scared to start a business in the first place. They are always willing to give advice on something they have never experienced. And why not, they have nothing to lose!! But you have the courage to venture out into the deep and give it a try. Yes it took courage that may have made others call you a FOOL. But that's a compliment!!

In the bible, there is a story about a leader named Gideon. Gideon was able to defeat an army of thousands with only 300 soldiers. (Judges 7:7-25) Gideon looked like a FOOL, but he was Following Only One Lead. God's lead!! That "One Lead" could be the mission that God put in your heart or an idea you wanted to try. I believe in experimenting!! I think that is what I like about being an entrepreneur most. In addition, if the business doesn't work, no money is loss but mine. I can definitely say I have NEVER had an unsuccessful business! I have walked away with money, wisdom or both. But I have never walked away with nothing. In my mind, that is success all the way around.

Experience is a great teacher and friend. As a teacher, your experiences will teach you what to do and what not to do. As a friend, your experience will comfort you when trouble hits or challenges come because you have been there before. That friendship with your experiences holds your hand in the storm and says "its ok, I'm here with you again."

In the midst of looking like a FOOL, you become the guide people look to when they want to pursue their dreams. It's amazing you only look like a FOOL for a minute and then you look like a hero. I think people want you to see if you sink first as they watch from the shore. But when you don't sink, they want your advice and help. I am all for helping, but why talk bad about me while you are on the shore watching?

THINK BIG THEN THINK SMALL

Please don't get caught up in the think big, go big theory. A lot have people have gotten a second mortgage on their homes because they were thinking big but didn't really think at all. You have to do some research before just jumping out there. Are you willing to risk the roof over your head for an idea that you couldn't afford? Or for an idea that wasn't thought out? Planning is important!! You don't have to plan so hard that you don't do anything. But plan enough to execute with minimal risk. If you are a family man/women, don't put your kids at risk over a feeling. Your feeling may leave them homeless and resenting you later when they grow older. Your family investment comes first!! No amount of money can replace family.

An entrepreneur is a person that organizes a business, assuming the risk for the sake of a profit. This definition does not tell how much the business should make or how big/small the business should be. If you have 100 employees or one employee, you are still a business!! If your business makes $100 million a year or $100 a year, you are still a business!! Don't think you have to leave your job to be an entrepreneur. This is a big misconception. If you put in 2 hours a week or 70 hours a week, you are still an entrepreneur. Some entrepreneurs prefer to work a full-time job and have a business. My grandfather and father taught me that this plan lowers the risk of losing your business and having nothing to fall back on. There is a lot pressure on being an entrepreneur and maintaining your life style based on your next sale. You can work a full-time job and be an entrepreneur with multiple businesses, I did!!

Having a big plan is OK. But after you have a big plan, figure out a small plan to test the waters. Try your business idea on a small scale. That doesn't mean you don't have faith in the business. That just means you are wise enough to know you have other responsibilities as well. I work as an engineer for a larger military contractor and I am also an entrepreneur. Having an engineering job benefits me financially as well as mentally. I don't have to worry about losing all I have worked for to go after a dream. My job teaches me about how large corporations do business. My job also teaches me about dealing with difficult situations and difficult people. I have learned when a conversation get's too heated, to lower my voice and talk slower. If tensions are high and adrenalin is flowing, your slower words give time for tempers to lower and anxieties to calm. My engineering job is like being in business school and I am taking all the notes I can.

If the scaled down version of your big plan goes well, you can take the leap and go further if you want. You may want to stay where you are because it is comfortable for now. Suppose the scaled down version is too much for you, you can back out with minimal loss. Your dream might be to start a restaurant. You may want to start selling dinners from home, from church or from a food cart first. See how much your food is desired. Also, you will see a small scale of dealing with different customer personalities, and constantly cooking and meeting the demand of your customers. After a sample, you may say that was too much for you. The good thing is you didn't go broke in the process. If you would have taken out a loan, you would have had to pay it back without income from your business. If you have the capital to go big and it will not impact you if you lose the money, then go big!! But I doubt you would decide to do that if you had the money. Nobody likes to lose money on purpose. To bless somebody with money is one thing, but to lose it is another.

"Just because it's convenient doesn't mean it's right for you."

YOU WANT ME TO INVEST WHAT??

It amazes me how people want you to invest in their company, but they have NO MONEY invested in their company. If that was the case, I would just take the business and make the company mine. I would use the person to sweep the floors when needed. You have to be your biggest investor!! People will invest in you if you have more to lose. You may not have the most money invested, but you have the most of YOU invested. That means you will push and work harder because you can't afford to lose.

People don't invest in lazy people!! People invest in hard workers. They want to see how driven you are. It's ok to start the car, but are you willing to take the car out of park and drive on the interstate? That's what investors want to see!! It's interesting how some people want to make money off other people's money. I know it sounds good, but its poor passion. If the business goes down, you have little to lose. You just close that business, find new investors and open another business. The drawback is you have not learned anything. When you are invested, you make sure you learn something, win or lose. So when you open the next business, you won't make the same mistakes over and over again. Experience is a good teacher if you are listening and willing to learn.

I am sharing this information with you so you can understand starting a business isn't that bad. It's running it and keeping it going that's the challenge!! But when challenges come, wisdom comes too. If you want people to invest in your business, you start investing in it first. Put in your time, energy, wisdom and yes, your MONEY!! That way, people won't say "you want me to invest in what?"

THE 24 HOURS THEORY

I have a quote that says, "The difference between a rich man and a poor man is what he does with his 24 hours." I have known this to be true, more times than not. A lot of people want to make money but aren't willing to put in the work to make the money. How many times have you heard someone say they want something someone else has while sitting on their behind? (I hope that's not you!!) The only way your business will be successful is if you are willing to put in the work, learning your business and cultivating your business. Yes you will make mistakes, but they aren't mistakes if you learn from them. In spite of what anyone says, having your own business is still work even if you enjoy it.

No matter what business you own, know there will be something you don't like about the business. This is a given, so tell yourself this before you start. This way when you encounter the part of being an entrepreneur you don't like, you were already prepared for it. You can say to yourself "this is what that crazy author was talking about!!" I am going to tell you a big misconception. People may have made you feel bad because you aren't an entrepreneur. People may have said if you are working for someone else, you could lose your job tomorrow. They don't tell you, if they lost their clients, they will be unemployed tomorrow too. Some entrepreneurs will say if they lose a few clients, they will still have some clients with some money coming in versus no money coming in at all. However, if you know how to save part of your income and aren't too proud to work in fast food or stock a warehouse until you find a better job, you will be ok. One mistake entrepreneurs make is they don't save. They have all their money locked in the business. I know you are wondering, "Is he trying to tell me not to be an entrepreneur?" No, I am making sure you are doing it for the right reasons. I don't want you to open a business because you bought into the "being an entrepreneur is so great" hype. It is great, but it's also a lot of great work.

For an entrepreneur, you have to work your 24-hours!! When other people are asleep, you have to work your plan or spend time thinking of a plan. When other people are watching the game, you have to make new contacts to keep your business going. When other people are out with their friends, you have to take some of that time and put in some work!! I am not saying entrepreneurs don't have fun, they do but in moderation. If you read the "Think Big Then Think Small" section of this book, you will understand how to manage getting started. Remember, God gave all of us 24 hours but what we do with it is up to us.

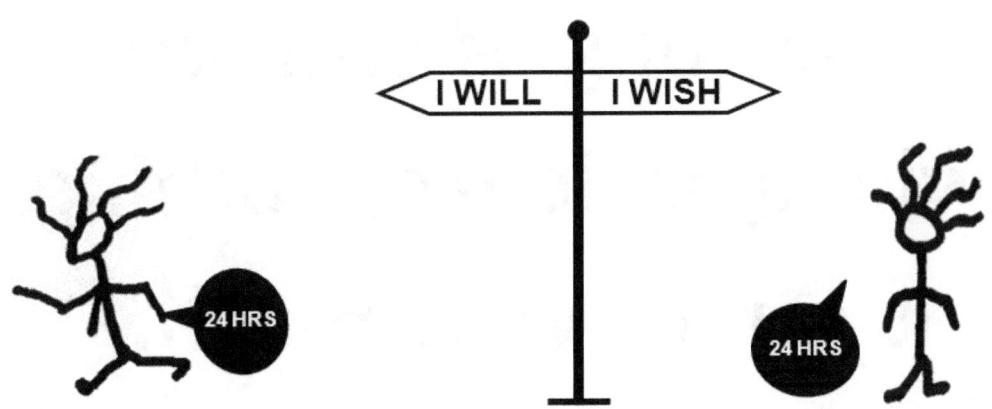

"As long as you are willing to learn, nothing is out of your reach."

ALWAYS OPEN

An entrepreneur is always on the job. Please don't think you are off!! You are always working even when you don't look like you are working. For example, you may be having a conversation with someone at a cookout and you discover they need a special service. Now the service they need is a service your company provides. It's time to clock in!! You have to be willing to work overtime, under-time and all-around-time. This is a part of being an entrepreneur!! If you can't handle that, don't be an entrepreneur or don't expect your business to be successful. I am not saying don't spend time with family or relax. No, you need that to balance YOU out. Just be willing to share information about your business at any time. I have had businesses I didn't even advertise (Not even in conversations). That was a sign I didn't need to be in that market. You should be so proud of your business that you are willing to tell the world.

When you aren't involved in activities related to your business, you may be setting up a meeting for future sales. If you want to expand your business or gain more sales, you need to have meetings with future clients. When I want to work with another non-profit, church or get my product in the store, I'll set up a meeting with the potential client. When I am making the appointment, it is not the time to talk about the details. That will come later. It is at the business meeting that I discuss any business concerns or answer any questions the client may have.

I would suggest you make the meeting short and easy for them. You should conduct the meeting at their business or in a relaxing environment such as coffee shop, beagle shop or perhaps a bookstore. This gets them away from their usual environment. Ask your client their availability on weekdays and weekends. After you find out that information, set the date as soon as possible. The quicker you meet, the quicker you are to your next opportunity.

Have you ever heard someone say that you need an elevator speech? That means you need to have a few lines to explain your business from the time you travel on an elevator from the 1st floor to 2nd floor. You never know, that elevator meeting may be the first business meeting that leads to future income.

On the this page, write down three words that describe what your business offers, even if the business is YOU. Then explain each word in one sentence. I will use me as an example. The three words for me are Motivational Speaker, Poet and Author. I perform motivational speeches and workshops on Relationships/Marriage, Personal Finances and Goal Planning. I am an inspirational poet and MC for open mics. I am the author of 5 books. Now it's your turn.

LIST YOUR WORDS

1. _____

2. _____

3. _____

EXPLAIN WORD #1

_____

_____

_____

EXPLAIN WORD #2

_____

_____

_____

EXPLAIN WORD #3

_____

_____

_____

Based on the information you have listed on the previous pages, you can develop this into an elevator speech. Memorize what you have written. First, memorize your three words (This is very important). Then memorize the explanation for each word. You don't have to memorize the explanation word-for-word, but you should have a clear understanding of what it means and how to say it. You don't want your explanation to sound stale and without passion. Just mentioning these few things in a conversation will lead to more questions and get people interested in what you do. At this point, you can get their phone number, discuss what they are looking for and how you can be of service to them. But this only works if you are always open.

"Just because it doesn't exist doesn't mean you can't create it."

OUT OF BUSINESS

Just because you have to close your business doesn't mean you are a failure. This was something I had to gradually learn. I have opened many businesses, but I have closed many businesses too. I remember when I shut down my first website, I was sick. I thought, "How can I ever manage another business if I couldn't manage this one?" Not to mention, I had two businesses at the time. Since then I have learned when you close one business, it leaves room for the next one. But you have to have learned something from the one you closed. I mentioned earlier in this book about never having an unsuccessful business. This is because I was willing to learn. From every business I had, I learned something. I learned what works for me and what doesn't work for me. I even learned new strategies from my previous business that I took into the next business.

I have a quote that says "A warrior always walks away with something." Whether a warrior wins the battle or loses, he always walks away with something. If he wins, he walks away with the plunder. If he loses, he walks away with what worked, what didn't work, a new plan and possibly some new techniques that he learned along the way. He even learns from the techniques that were used on him. You have to take this ability on if you want to be an entrepreneur. From the ashes of your business closing may be the birth of a new business. All isn't lost Warrior!! Your first business may not be the one that's most successful for you. It may be the second one. Or even still, the third, fourth or fourteenth!! I know some of you didn't like the last line but it is true. Me personally, I enjoy starting businesses and learning from them. So no matter how many I may open or close, I just enjoy the experience of trying something new and learning from it. I don't think of it as what I lost, but the investment I made in myself and what I learned along the way. I guess that's my entrepreneurial spirit.

GIVE IT AWAY

One thing I have learned is if you give something away, that gesture will lead to more sales. I will give you an example. Have you ever been in the food court of the mall or in a grocery store and they are giving away free samples. The point is for you to try it and hopefully you will enjoy the product and buy the product. Now there is always going to be a person who takes advantage of that, but that's not the point. The sample you give may lead to a customer for life. People are less willing to spend their money and take a chance, but they will take a free chance. The little bit you invest in samples may payoff richly later.

When I go out and speak, sometime I give a book or two away. One reason is to invest in someone's life but the other is to show everyone in the room I have a product. People in the audience ask the receiver if they can see the book, and that preview may turn into another sale. And of course, if one person buys, another will want to buy. A busy vending table usually means a paid vending table. When many people are surrounding the author, others want to know what the commotion is about and they want to be a part of it. If you can figure out a creative way to give away a sample of your product, do so!! Even if it's putting exerts from your book on your blog or facebook.

If you have a barber shop, offer half price haircuts on a certain day of the week and see what happens. It may not be a free sample, but it's a good sample. If free offers break your piggy bank, then discount it on a Customer Appreciation Day. Tell your regular customers to invite someone new and their next haircut will be half price. Your customer may treat someone to a free haircut and that person becomes your new customer. The key is to think outside the box, but find what works best for you. This is your business so you have the right to determine what fits.

"Leaders don't follow everyone else, so why are you?"

DRESS AHEAD

Have you heard people say you should dress for where you are going? I fully agree!! You have to take your business serious or other people won't. You may have a business where you are the only employee today, but you should dress like you have over 100 employees. This may be the reality of your tomorrow, so why not look like it today. This also reflects confidence in where you are going. People take well-dressed and well-manicured people serious. The Robert J. Trulaske, Sr. College of Business tells men "Do wear your suit jacket when you conduct business outside your office. Your authority travels with you." (Professional Dress) The coat represents your authority in your business. It shows that you are in control and determined in your business. I am not saying you have to wear a suit and tie at every meeting, because our society has embraced a more casual business atmosphere today. But it doesn't hurt!!

Always speak in terms of "we" for your business. That makes people think the company is big even if it's just you. The mission for my first business was "We write life for you." The "we" was me and God. I figured if I had Him, I had a team like no other. It is ok to say and it is not misleading. Saying "we" made the business seem huge. Take yourself serious in order to be taken serious. Men, put on a shirt and tie for that meeting you have about your business. Ladies, put on that dress or pants suit for your future clients. Even if the job requires you to dress down, you can still dress up for the meeting. You will be your own Sales Team or Manager.

If you had a sales team, wouldn't you want them to look their best if they were representing your company? Well you are the sales team representing your company so do the same as you would expect someone else to do. When I have meeting for speaking engagements, I feel like I am the "client" and the "booking manager". In the booking manager role, I show up with a shirt and tie for the meeting. In the client role, I show up with jeans and a T-shirt to speak at the youth event.

Dressing ahead also prepares you mentally. You start to feel like you are somebody, and you are!! You are the right person for your destiny. Dress like it and feel like it. No one can be YOU or sell YOU better than you. Dress ahead for where you are going and don't stay stuck where you are.

I HEARD ABOUT YOU

Your greatest sales tactic will always be word of mouth. With this being said, you have to treat your customers right. It's sad to say that bad news travels quicker than good news, but it's true. People will talk about your bad service before they talk about your good service. First, don't get on the "bad service" list. In this case, no news is good news. Second, to get on the "good service" path, start by saying "Thank You" to all your customers. Such a small phrase goes a long way!! Instead of closing a deal with just "good bye", end with a "Thank you for your support and Have a good day". People love to be praised and to feel important. If you offer them that, they will come back.

Never start a shouting match with a customer. This never ends well. You may win the argument but lose other customers or potential customers that were there listening. Always say, "Thank you" even if your customers are wrong. YES, I said even if they are wrong!! There is a polite way to say anything. You can say "Thank you for your comments/suggestions, but we are not in a position to honor that request at this time." Now that's a nice way to say NO!! Also, make sure you and your customers are on the same page. Repeat what you think they are requesting back to them. Otherwise, you will waste time working diligently and successfully on the wrong product or service. Ask plenty of questions and answer plenty of questions. Then, ask them if they have any more questions. Why am I asking you to do this? Think about how you would feel if you were waiting patiently and received the wrong thing. Why give your customers that experience?

If you are not a people person, you may want to hire someone who is. Or if one of your employers is a people person, put them on the frontline and play to their strengths. Just because you aren't the best in dealing with people doesn't mean you are a horrible entrepreneur. It just means you may need to improve a weakness (We ALL have weaknesses) or that you need another resource to fulfill a need. The cheapest way is to get better at it, but it takes time. If you can't do that, get someone else. Either way you choose leaves a better impression on the customer. This way when someone says "I heard about you" it will be good news.

"Your dream coming to past may not be tied to money, but tied to resources (people)."

IDEAS THAT DIDN'T WORK

My wife laughed at me when she found a piece of paper that I typed up called "Ideas that did work." I had listed businesses or programs that didn't do well. For a while, I didn't mention the ideas that didn't work. I would just push them to the back of my mind like they didn't exist. One day, I remember hearing someone say, "Everyone has had ideas that didn't do well." Since I like to face my fears (Fears hold you back from progress), I decided to list them. I will admit I had been brainwashed to believe that when you write certain things down, you are acknowledging you are a failure. This is so far from the truth!! Thomas Watson founder of IBM said "Double your rate of failure. You're thinking of failure as the enemy of success. But it isn't at all. You can be discouraged by failure or you can learn from it. So go ahead and make mistakes. Make all you can. Because, remember that's where you'll find success." (Inspiration)

As I listed the ideas, the fear began to lessen and I kept on typing. Like anything you fear, I was scared when I typed the first one, but I kept on typing in fear. After my list was complete, I began to laugh. I laughed so hard tears began to fall. The joke was, I remembered the time and thought, "What was I thinking?" On the other hand, the event itself was a comedy moment. My fear actually brought me joy!! There is a verse in the bible that states "...and the truth shall set you free", and it did. (John 8:32) From that experience, I learned we will all have ideas that won't go as planned, but you can laugh about them later.

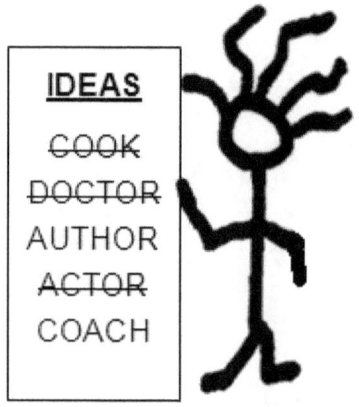

LIST OF IDEAS THAT DIDN'T WORK

On this page, I want you to list ideas that didn't work. This exercise may give you a laugh and help you get over the feeling of failure that accompanies ideas that didn't work. So go ahead and start listing.

1. _____

2. _____

3. _____

4. _____

5. _____

6. _____

7. _____

8. _____

9. _____

10. _____

"BUT WAIT, THERE'S MORE!!"

When I watch TV, all I see is great Success,
I want to be rich, I want to have lots of money, I want to be one of the best.
The Preachers are even talking about prosperity and all that I can have,
As I look around me, I want that prosperity now!!

"But wait, there's more!!"

People have told me that being an entrepreneur is the way to do it,
All I had to do was start a business and I would be in it to win it.
Quick money, quick fast, that's what I want,
I am going to get mine so I can have a big house and a fancy car to flaunt.

"But wait, there's more!!"

Yet no one told me being an entrepreneur meant it
takes money to make money,
It seemed like after all the paperwork, licenses and business
fees I was losing money.
I thought I could buy some real estate and that's it,
I didn't know I had to work so hard to find dependable
tenants and have good credit.

"But wait, there's more!!"

And that network marketing scheme was a gimmick too,
I didn't know I had to hustle everyday and increase my sells to get to level two.
And the main people that gave me advice, never even had a business, owned
real estate or went door-to-door,
I guess I will plan and be content for now instead of listening to those
commercials that say "But wait, there's more!!"

"Don't give up on who you can be by just settling for who you currently are."

ENTREPRENEURS ADAPT

If you are in a business and your current plan isn't working, you can change directions. You are the CEO!! If you don't have the power to do so, who does? You are not admitting to being a failure if you change the direction of your business. Actually, it is very wise!! When I had a business renting conference room space, my suite also had a few small offices as well. The office space rentals were consistently profitable, but the profitability of my conference room rentals were hit or miss. Unlike the office space rental, someone always had to be present to rent the conference rooms. Consequently, I decided to focus on renting office space instead. I negotiated a deal to change my suite to one that offered multiple office spaces instead. This was a great idea!! However, I eventually closed the business.

After I closed my business, the owners of the office building began using my idea to rent office space. TD Jakes had a term called "Reposition" in his book "Reposition Yourself." (Jakes, 2007) It meant to find out where you were and go another route for better results. This is what you have to do if Plan A doesn't work. Reposition and create a Plan B or maybe a Plan C or D. If you are passionate about the business, try a new approach until you find a groove that works for you.

I have learned that entrepreneurs adapt to the circumstances they face. You can tell if the business is for you if you are willing to stick in there during the highs and lows of the business. I didn't say go broke and lose your shirt though!! If you are out of ideas and have no desire to change, you may want to close the business. I also mentioned closing a business in this book as well. You don't want the business to stress you to the point your health becomes an issue. Sometimes adapting means you should leave the business and move on. You can always open another business in which you are passionate about. Why waste your energy in a business you are no longer interested in, or worse a business that's draining you. You can take that same energy into a new business that is in your heart and thrive!! Business can be like a bad relationship. If the business is taking joy from your life, it may be time to end the relationship.

LEAD TO CREATE LEADERS

In a business, you want to create leaders. However, the only way to create leaders is to be willing to let them lead. With the right training, you have some great leaders already working with you. Let's go a little further about leadership. You have to be a good leader to create good leaders. The bible explains that a leader must become a servant. (Luke 22:26) How can you be a leader if you don't want to serve anyone? You want the people who work with you to look up to you as a semi god figure. That is not leadership!! That is idolatry!! Leaders have to want to see their people succeed and grow. A leader not only wants to see his employees succeed and grow, but he is also willing to give them the skills and resources to do so.

Let the people that work with you see what you do. This way they can be aware of the challenges you face and how you deal with them. Teach them how you deal with conflict, customers and companies of which you are partners. Also, be open to their ideas. Their ideas may give you a way to grow your business. Be willing to try some of their ideas. If the idea doesn't fit your business, don't use it but encourage them to continue giving ideas. Think of other ways you can use employees' ideas. Find out what part of the business they would like to learn. Nothing is like a person who desires to learn. If you teach them, they will be able to take some of the workload off your shoulders. This will give you more time to relax or create new business relationships and opportunities.

One rumor is, if you train the people that work for you, they will take your position. In a way, that is what you want as an entrepreneur!! You want employees that can run the business while you aren't around. Some people also think if you tell too much, the workers will start their own business. I wouldn't worry about that because no one can do your business like you. They can duplicate it, but it will never be like yours. Moreover, longevity in business is connected to passion, not trying to get rich. If they are trying to get rich quick, their business will soon fall off when the first storm hits. You need to know how to ride out storms and even play in the storm every once in a while.

Understand these rumors are usually started by people who never had a business or people who gave up on their business. Don't let these rumors stop you from being a leader that creates leaders.

"If you don't keep moving toward what's important to you, time will move it further away from you."

WHAT MONEY!!

Some people say business is all about making money. I don't believe that is true. A business is about making money for yourself or a cause, but there has to be a deeper reason. Like I said before, you have to like the business you are in. Entrepreneur A.G. Gaston said, "I never went into anything with the idea of making money...I thought of doing something, and it would come up and make money. I never thought of trying to get rich." (A. G. Gaston, 2008) Impassionate pursuits kill the longevity of business. But let's get back to the money!! Just like budgeting for your house, you have to budget for your business. If you are taking out loans and getting investors involved, that is one thing. However, you need to also think about how you are going to pay the loan or investors back if the business doesn't work. By the way, it is hard for a small business to get a loan. The business has to establish some credit first.

One banker said a good way to establish credit is by getting a department store credit card or a bank credit card for your company. Trust me, as soon as you get your business name registered, the credit card offers will start coming in!! Buy small items needed for the company and keep paying the credit card off. The more the bank can trust you with their money, the more willing they are to give you more. After a while, the bank will raise your credit limit and possibly grant you a business loan. Once the bank increases your limit, that doesn't mean go crazy and spend more money. Be mindful that going on a spending spree can ruin your company's credit as well. The credit card plan is not a good idea if you already have credit card problems in your personal life. You may use the same philosophy with your business card as you do with your personal card. This will create more trouble than it's worth. Personally, I did not get a credit card for any of my businesses. I know how undisciplined I have been with my personal credit cards, so I try to avoid credit cards in my businesses.

Earlier in this book, I mentioned thinking big then thinking small. This is a good way to manage and budget your risks. When I start my businesses, I am the first investor. I calculate how much it will cost to start the business on a small scale and then I save the capital. That way, the profit will be mine if it goes well and I don't owe anyone if the business goes downhill. Like any investment, never invest more than you are willing to lose. There are shows on TV about people investing their life savings in a stock that has an unreal interest rate. All along it was a ponzy scheme and the people lost everything. Don't let this happen to you when it comes to your business. Plan wisely when it comes to financial management.

Another important component of your business is the pricing of your product. If you don't have any idea what to charge, see what other businesses are charging for a similar product or service. If your product is unique, find a business close to what you are doing and use their pricing as a guideline for what you charge. Experts say charge twice as much as you think the price should be because we usually short change ourselves. I believe you can charge what you feel. This is your business!! If you want to charge double or triple, do so. You are the one that has to live with the results. Another thing you want to keep in mind is the target market or audience to whom you are selling your product or service. Will they pay that price? It's sad to say, but depending on the product, some people will pay more for something they can't afford. Not everyone can afford a $100 pair of shoes or a $200 purse, but they find a way.

I laugh when people talk about the economy and how times are so tight. I have learned that people will spend money on what they want, regardless of the condition of the economy. I don't believe a tight economy applies to you if you are still making the same amount of money. Taxes will always go up!! Alcohol sales will always be good no matter what is happening with the economy. Some people may go from purchasing top shelf alcohol to medium shelf, but they will still purchase. Some people will keep buying the latest cell phones even if it means paying their rent late. So price your product wisely and if they want it bad enough, they will pay for it.

Always find ways to negotiate the right price for services you require or products you need for your business. In bulk purchases such as T-shirts, the more you buy the cheaper they are. If you need a service multiple times a year, see if you can negotiate a better service package or create one price based on your business' budget. Just like in a marriage, "Negotiate, Negotiate, Negotiate!! There has to be some kind of compromise that can be made. Or there may be a company that can provide the same service cheaper and sometimes better. Ask people in your industry who they use for their services or products. Small business owners like to help other small business owners. They understand you are trying to survive and make a better living for yourself too.

Once you have saved all this money negotiating and making great sales, reinvest a portion back into your company. If you sale 100 books, save some of your profits to buy more books or publish your next book. Don't go shopping like its Christmas and spend all that you have earned. I know you are saying that is common sense, but you would be shocked how often this happens. It takes money to keep a business or organization going. Spending it all is not an option. Also, don't spend all your money on advertising. Advertising does work, but if it comes down to an advertising spot or your lease payment, it's best to pay your lease. Otherwise you will finally get some customers one month later, but you will have no building or business in which to service them. Just like in your personal life, you try to buy on sale and save money. Do the same in your business. If not, you will wind up looking at your business account balance and wonder "what happened to all the money!!"

"Run your race at your pace."

THE BIRTH OF POETIC SOULS INC

I have had many businesses but the one business that has stood the test of time is my non-profit business called "Poetic Souls Inc." The philosophy behind this business is giving, PERIOD!! In that, Poetic Souls Inc has blessed me to see so many of my dreams come true. The business has not made millions of dollars but it has made me feel like a billionaire. Poetic Souls Inc has a mission of "Inspiring the world through poetry..." The "..." means it is still growing in how it will continue to inspire the world. Poetic Souls Inc has touched many lives and is still touching lives as you read this book. As a matter of fact, the profits from every book I sell from Poetic Souls Inc. goes to reinvest in making a difference in the world. Only God knows what's next.

In 2004, I started having open mics at my house. For those who may not be familiar with what an open mic is, it is an event where poets can come and share their poetry with each other. It is not just limited to poetry, but also music. I had noticed I was surrounded by inspirational poets. I thought it would be a perfect time to put together an open mic event outside my home environment. Since I had hosted (I was the Master of Ceremonies) an open mic before, I had some experience. At the time, there were not many ongoing faith-based open mics in my area. I wanted to have one, but I didn't have the funds to rent a venue. So what did I do, I had a conversation with God since HE has all the connections. In my kitchen, I told God that I wanted to do an open mic but I couldn't rent space due to my lack of funds. God responded by telling me to do the open mic at churches. That way I would not have to pay for the space. With that, I said I would pay for food to feed the people since the space will be free. Being the budget conscious person I am, I knew I could feed the people with very little money. I also figured that I could do a dollar donation bucket at the door so the church would reap some financial benefit. I didn't want to charge God's people, so whatever they could give would do. With this agreement and plan, I moved forward. The next day I decided to entitle the open mic sessions, "Poetic Souls."

Now the next challenge was to find a church to have the open mic session. However, I didn't think that would be a challenge. I started by asking the leadership in the church I attended at the time, but that ended with a NO! I couldn't understand why they wouldn't want to do something that was for God's people. But what doesn't kill you makes you stronger. So I ventured on to ask other churches and I heard NO after NO. I was actually knocking on church doors and talking with secretaries trying to get this open mic event off the ground. After enough No's, you will eventually get frustrated even if it is for God's people.

One day while at work, I was venting to a co-worker and friend of mine, Fernando Gaines, about how I couldn't find a location for Poetic Souls. As I was venting, Fernando asked me questions about how Poetic Souls worked and what it involved. I proceeded to tell him not thinking he would be interested. I also didn't know he was a minister of a local church named "Faith Temple Holiness Church" in Portsmouth, VA. Later that night, Fernando called me with more questions. At this point, I began to wonder why he was asking so many questions. Fernando told me he would ask his Bishop, Bishop Juanelle Johnson, if Poetic Souls could be held there. Later on that night, Fernando called me and asked those sweet words "So when do you want to have the first open mic?" WOW!!! It still sends chills down my spine!!

Poetic Souls had a location and a date for its first event. Staying true to my agreement with God, I created a budget and provided food. The day of the event was exciting yet full of fear and stress. I didn't know what to expect!! To make matters worse, the musician that I had scheduled to perform couldn't make it. I told Fernando and he said he had someone at the church that could play keyboard. I found out later that the person he was referring to was him. Before I got to the church, a poet I least expected to come was already at the church asking if I needed him to help. What a blessing!! His name was Jason Austin. He would become one of the main faces I would share the stage with. When I arrived at the church, the other poets I expected didn't show, but Jason was there. As the people began to arrive, I was getting more and more nervous but this is what I asked for and why I worked so hard. It was time to start and all I had was my poems and Jason, but that's all I needed. For the rest of the night, Jason and I hosted and read from our notebooks until the night was over. We poured out our souls in a whirl-wind of emotions. The audience laughed, cried and even worshipped God in moments of His presence. The people in the audience even sung in between poems. It was a night I would never forget!! We had found something that had never been tapped into before. The next thing I knew the night was over and the first Poetic Souls was behind me.

After that first night, I began to meet with other churches and word spread about the Poetic Souls Open Mic. We began to get invited to other churches and non-profit organizations to perform and even MC other open mics. Every time Poetic Souls hosted an open mic, I made sure the dollar donation bucket was available and food was available too. Some organizations gave us the dollar donation bucket back with whatever was donated and some organizations would pay us above and beyond what was donated. The donations began to cover the food and Poetic Souls was self sustaining. The Poetic Souls family grew with poets such as Lisa J (my wife), Madonna Rose, Venus, Testimony, Paula Norman, Kiki, Walt Love, Othella and of course Jason Austin. Poetic Souls has performed at different events throughout the East Coast.

Poetic Souls began doing interviews on the radio and even reciting poetry over the air. I was overwhelmed when Bishop Johnson asked me to represent Poetic Souls as part of his radio talk show "Church Talk in the Barbershop". Every month we would record 3 shows at a time and I would recite the poem of the day (good times!!). The show aired for at least 3 years. Poetic Souls then evolved into doing poetry workshops, men's events and women's events. The money was coming in as donations for the service we provided. Mind you, we did not charge for any of our services!! This was all by the grace of God moving his people to give. This allowed Poetic Souls to travel and perform on the East Coast, all funded by donations. As poetic Souls grew, I incorporated the organization and changed the name to Poetic Souls Inc (PSI). Poetic Souls Inc began to make CD's and inspirational T-shirts. The sales from these products created more revenue to pursue our mission.

As I expanded in my gift, Poetic Souls Inc expanded in the services it offered. I published my first book in 2010, *Life is a Motivational Speech*, under the Poetic Soul Inc name. *Filthy Rags, Single Again,* and *The CHEAPS* followed my first book. Workshops and motivational speeches were birthed from my books. The book sales paid for event space, workshop materials and other expenses used to inspire others. All workshops and speeches Poetic Souls Inc performs are free of change, but open to donations.

Poetic Souls Inc is still running strong using this model. The organization is advancing in new territories to inspire, empower and help people make better decisions in their lives. Once again, the source and success of Poetic Souls Inc is giving. The bible says if you give unto others it will be given unto you even more. (Luke 6:38) Poetic Souls Inc believes these gifts are freely given by God and now freely given unto the world. (Matthew 10:8) I will admit, these Poetic Souls Inc principles don't make too much sense based on the usual business mottos, but it produces by faith. I will continue to stick to these Poetic Souls Inc principles and hope others will follow suit. My desire is that many will see how blessed they can be if they pursue their passion with faith and not just the pursuit of money.

"Being the best is not a requirement for success, but having the courage to try is."

BIBLIOGRAPHY

A. G. Gaston. 2008. <http://en.wikipedia.org/wiki/A._G._Gaston>.

Chatzky, Jean. *Money Rules: The Simple Path to Lifelong Security*. Rodale Books , 2012.

Inspiration. n.d. <http://failureclub.org/inspiration/>.

Jakes, T.D. *Reposition Yourself: Living Life Without Limits*. Simon and Schuster Inc., 2007.

James, Geoffrey. *10 Dumb Sales Tactics to Avoid*. 7 September 2012. <http://www.inc.com/geoffrey-james/10-dumb-sales-tactics-to-avoid.html>.

Lindner, Melanie. *What To Look For In A Business Partner*. 28 April 2008. <http://www.forbes.com/2008/04/28/google-apple-partnership-ent-hr-cx_ml_0428pickapartner.html>.

Professional Dress. n.d. <http://business.missouri.edu/programs-and-admissions/undergraduate/student-development/business-career-services/professional-dress>.

Stanley, Thomas J. *Networking with the Affluent*. McGraw-Hill, 1997.

Watson, Emily. *John B. Watson*. 1999. <http://www.muskingum.edu/~psych/psycweb/history/watson.htm>.

Other Books by Ryan "Jenks" Jenkins

"Life is a Motivational Speech" © 2010

"Filthy Rags: Everybody is Fighting Something" © 2011

"Single Again: Friendships, Relationships & Marriage" © 2012

"The CHEAPS: Why Spend It If You Don't Have To" © 2012

Books are available to purchase online at
www.PoeticSoulsInc.com

www.ingramcontent.com/pod-product-compliance
Lightning Source LLC
Chambersburg PA
CBHW071816170526
45167CB00003B/1329